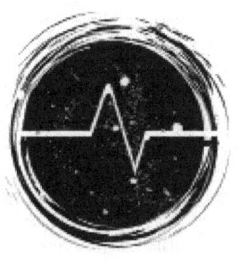

WELCOME BACK, LAZARUS

*Getting Your Footing Back
after a Near-Death Experience*

Robbie Grayson III

©Robert W. Grayson III
All rights reserved.
2022

No part of this book may be used or reproduced by any means: graphic, electronic, or mechanical, including photocopying, recording, taping or by any information storage retrieval system without the written permission of the author except in the case of brief quotations embodied in critical articles and reviews. Because of the dynamic nature of the Internet, any web addresses or links contained in this book may have changed since publication and may no longer be valid. Although every precaution has been taken to verify the accuracy of the information contained herein, the author and publisher assume no responsibility for any errors or omissions so that no liability is assumed for damages that may result from the use of information contained within. The views expressed in this work are solely those of the author and do not necessarily reflect the views of the publisher whereby the publisher hereby disclaims any responsibility for them.

ATTRIBUTIONS
Interior Text Font: Minion Pro
Cover Design & Typesetting: Robbie W, Grayson III
Additional Credits on Credits Page

BOOK PUBLISHER INFORMATION
Traitmarker Books
www.traitmarkerbooks.com
traitmarker@gmail.com

Printed in United States of America

Table of Contents

A Note from the Publisher (iv)

The Purpose of This Book (v)

I. Lights Out | 9

II. Euphoria | 28

III. Lazarus, Come Forth | 45

IV. Back | 58

V. Aftermath | 82

Outro: Where You Go From Here | 119

Credits

About the Author

Contact

A Note
from the Publisher

The publisher is providing this book and its contents on an "as is" basis and makes no representations or warranties of any kind with respect to this book or its contents and disclaims all such representations and warranties, including but not limited to warranties of mental healthcare for a particular purpose.

The content of this book is for informational purposes only and is not intended to diagnose, treat, cure, or prevent any mental condition or disease. This book is not intended as a substitute for consultation with a licensed practitioner. Please consult with a physician or healthcare specialist regarding the suggestions and recommendations made in this book.

Traitmarker Media, LLC

The Purpose
of This Book

This little book is about my near-death experience and what I learned from it. First, it's difficult but necessary to develop a healthy appreciation for your own mortality before you die. Second, it's more difficult to try wrapping your head around the imminence of death while dying. Third, it's entirely another level of difficulty to complete the act of death and come back from it.

I originally thought myself to be in the second category: trying to wrap my head around the mere minutes I had left to live. I held that position for about a year until I finally acknowledged what my body had been trying to tell me all along: that I was in the third category.

Though I didn't complete the act of dying, I've been told that it was close. Even those who actually die for a period of time and later revive refer to that experience as *near death*. What's most important here is that the body doesn't discriminate a near-death experience by how many seconds or minutes away it was from death. I'm now of the opinion that if you required any intervention that brought you back from the brink of death, your body simply considers that you died and behaves accordingly.

Drawing the artificial distinction between "dead" and "almost dead" for almost a year wore me down to the nub for reasons I'll mention in this book. For now, here's what was key to my near-death experience:

- I *thought* I was going to die
- I *fought* to stay alive
- I *lost consciousness* fighting

And here's the clincher that warranted my writing this little book in the first place:

- When I awoke almost 30 hours later, *I was disappointed to be alive.*

Remember that last sentence while you read this book because it's the hinge upon which every page of this book turns.

For the time that I was unconscious, however, I was in an in-between state from which I couldn't wake myself though I tried. But that's not the point of this little book. The point is that it was the coming back that was harder than the going out.

After being back for a few weeks, the story of Lazarus came to mind in an almost sardonic way. I had always assumed that Lazarus was as happy as his sisters to be back from the dead. But I had never before considered what might have been Lazarus's point of view. It's not written.

However, it's possible that he wasn't as excited. He had, after all, been dead for three days. And dying is hard work. There's the intense denial that rouses manic energy to reverse the inevitable flow of events. There's the paralyzed thought that gets stuck bringing sense to the situation. There's the final movements that eke out as uncontrollable thrashing or a seizure. Then it's "lights out" with no recollection later on when the lights went out.

But coming back can be harder. All the fear, unhinging, confusion, decay, and disintegration happens again but in reverse. So, *Welcome Back, Lazarus* serves as a guide for friends and families of loved ones who have had close calls with death, found themselves alive again, but can't seem to get back into their former groove.

Robbie Grayson III,
Traitmarker Books
Franklin, Tennessee | March 2022

*I didn't stop to ask, Pooh.
Even at the very bottom of the river
I didn't stop to say to myself, 'Is this a Hearty
Joke, or is it the Merest Accident?'
I just floated to the surface,
and said to myself, 'It's wet.'*

A.A. MILNE

CHAPTER 1

Lights Out

Welcome Back, Lazarus

On May 14, 2016, I awoke with an upset stomach around 3:00 a.m. After getting out of bed and entering the downstairs bathroom, I had a sneezing fit. Almost three dozen sneezes, if I recall correctly.

That's when I felt *it* happen.

Robbie Grayson III

I THOUGHT THAT I WAS GOING TO DIE

Welcome Back, Lazarus

It's hard to describe the imminent feeling of death when you've no reference for it. But several things happened at once. The sum total effect was that I knew that I was dying. It wasn't a knowing that was in my head. It was in my gut.

- *Heat rose up my back*
- *My breathing changed*
- *My eyes burned*

You know what it's like to *really* know something without the aid of your brain? It might be imperceptible to logic (or the brain is slow to learn), but the body, if you listen to it, knows immediately.

What confirmed to me that my condition was terminal were two factors I had never before experienced:

- *It happened instantly*
- *I smelled decay*

No, I didn't intellectually understand that I was having anaphylaxis. It was suddenly onset. Like a sucker punch. Or an assault.

I was incinerating inside. And upon my first attempt at a deep breath, I inhaled what might have been the smell of a dumpster. These two factors escalated my panic, making it impossible for me to strike a calm frame of mind that would allow me a reprieve.

I knew that I needed to get my breathing under control if I had a chance to live, but the burning in my eyes and the ominous smell of death intensified and my anxiety spiraled out of my control.

Being an asthmatic since the age of eleven, I've had bouts with sudden anaphylaxis. But they were all manageable. None were vicious like this one.

The anaphylaxis came out of nowhere. It shot up my back from my waist to my neck, and the internal heat from losing oxygen pulsated inside me. The heat tried to get out and created an uncomfortable pins-and-needles sensation in my skin.

I felt its grip everywhere at once and had a fleeting image of an entity squeezing the air out of my lungs.

All of this happened in a matter of seconds, I think. During this time, I understood that I would die today:

- *In the next few minutes*
- *At this address*
- *In these clothes (my underwear)*
- *In the bathroom*
- *Alone*

I was slipping fast and found myself momentarily fixated on the right vertical trim of the bathroom door. It was my visual anchor to the world. I clung to it like my sanity depended on it while I simultaneously tried to wrap my head around the fact that I would be no more within a matter of minutes.

Not today. Please, not today.

Welcome Back, Lazarus

Suddenly, I felt the claustrophobia of dying alone in the bathroom, and I wanted nothing more than to live. Or be with others. I ran outside the bathroom to grab my inhaler and brought it back into the bathroom to use.

Nothing.

I ran into the laundry room to grab my nebulizer and brought it back into the bathroom to use.

Nothing.

Suddenly, I realized that I needed to get out of the bathroom altogether and out of the house to get air. Fumbling with the skeleton key in the front door of the antebellum, I stumbled out onto the porch to get a deep breath.

May in Tennessee is humid, uncomfortably warm, and pollen heavy.

Nothing again.

Welcome Back, Lazarus

At this point, I was groggy with asphyxiation and knew that I was only minutes away from the end of life. I was also aware at this point that it was too late for me to call 911. I live on a farm, and MapQuest usually takes people to a field about a mile behind the house.

It's over.

Robbie Grayson III

IT'S
OVER

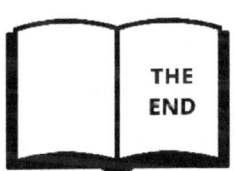

Welcome Back, Lazarus

I didn't have enough breath to formulate much of a sentence, but I knew that I had to alert my wife for several entangled reasons:

- *She needed to know what was happening to me*
- *She needed to call the ambulance, because I knew that she couldn't help me at this point. And what would she do with my body?*
- *I needed to hear her voice and know that she knew what I knew: that I knew I was dying*

Before I could get to her, I was aware that my daughter upstairs was awake and calling downstairs to find out if everything was OK. She had heard me open the front door and the sound of erratic movement downstairs. When I heard her voice, something energized me to want to live all the more.

Welcome Back, Lazarus

So saying it loud enough for both my wife and daughter to hear, I pounded on my bedroom door and eked out with what I thought was my last breath, *Call 911.*

I didn't even have it within me to use an exclamation point. My wife stirred, and that was the last thing I remember.

*The world
is quiet here.*

LEMONY SNICKET

CHAPTER 2

EUPHORIA

I would be cheating you if I were to describe the events told to me later of what was happening all around me at the time that I lost consciousness. I don't remember any of it (at least not in a conscious way), so none of it is the story I want to share. I want to share with you what I "remember."

What happened to me next was a conscious lapse of approximately 30 hours that felt like... forever maybe?

LETTING

GO

And here is where my story gets a little tricky in its telling because my memory took the form of physical sensation, not conscious thought.

After considering how to use words without lying to describe what for me was a wordless experience, I've fallen back on a device I learned as a child called *dynamic equivalence*. In a situation where it's impossible to translate a sentence word-for-word, you translate the feeling or intent in an equivalent way.

Welcome Back, Lazarus

Having grown up abroad, I'm familiar with the value of translating the words of one language into the feelings of another. Saying something in English to someone who doesn't understand it doesn't help with understanding. And raising your voice louder and louder each time gets you nowhere.

But throw in a gesture for emphasis, and you get a little closer. Use your eyes, and you get even closer. In short, a great number of experiences can be communicated more or less in this way.

So I'll translate the simplest word and idea bank that I can into feelings and sensations.

Robbie Grayson III

Welcome Back, Lazarus

While I was under, I believed I had died. Better yet, I assumed I was dead, which meant that I had no memories, thoughts, or concerns about the life I had just left and apparently was fine with it.

It's important to understand the difference between this and, say, suicide. I didn't premeditate my own death, consent to it early on, or cause it to happen while I was conscious. I blacked out while fighting to stay alive. However, I participated while under. This is an issue that caused me problems later on

I don't remember a second or a moment when it happened, but at some point after I lost consciousness I gave into the vortex of events that were sucking me under. I leaned into the direction that gravity was pulling me. Think about any sudden situation that requires your automatic reflex:

- *You trip*
- *You get startled*
- *Something gets close to your eye*
- *You bump into someone*
- *You choke*

Each threat requires of you an involuntary response. Why? Probably because one part of you is looking out for the other part of you. On an uninvestigated level, however, it just is.

For me there was no reflex. At some point I stopped looking out for the other part of me:

- *I didn't catch myself*
- *I didn't jump up*
- *I didn't blink*
- *I didn't pull back*
- *I didn't cough*

I didn't care anymore.

And
this
caused
me
serious
problems
later
on.

Welcome Back, Lazarus

When my body made the decision to let go—it wasn't a conscious decision that I made with my brain—it brought me an immediate sense of relief. After all, I had been up against a losing battle and used up every resource I had to keep from dying. What I gave just wasn't enough, and "it" won.

Considering what I had been through before losing consciousness, the only way I can describe the physical feeling involved in letting go is euphoria.

But there were layers of things that I had to let go to get to this point:

- *Alerting my wife and daughter that I was in danger*
- *Failing to take in a deep breath of air outside*
- *Unlocking the front door to get outside*
- *Failing to get my nebulizer to work*
- *Failing to get my inhaler to work*
- *Experiencing the immediate onset of anaphylaxis*
- *Having a sneezing fit*

Welcome Back, Lazarus

All of that was immediately obvious to me—to my conscious brain. But there was more that I was letting go than just that. It involved the things that happened before it:

- *Walking to the bathroom at 3 a.m.*
- *Awaking to an upset stomach*
- *Falling asleep late*
- *Getting the kids to bed*
- *Getting the dishes done*
- *Having the kids' busdriver, Ms. Barbara, over for dinner*

But then it was *much* more than that. It involved life patterns that were but faint recollections in my head at my losing consciousness:

- *Cleaning the house*
- *Driving the kids back and forth to work*
- *Picking up my littlest from the bus stop*
- *Publishing books*
- *Advising clients*
- *Working out*
- *Taking care of the house and property*
- *Traveling abroad*
- *Watching Netflix and Hulu*

After losing consciousness, I was aware that I was "still holding on." But to what and for what? At that point, I wasn't sure, and this is another issue that caused me problems later.

Almost as if it were a faint memory of a memory of yet another memory, my holding on lost sight of my original motivations for holding on. And, though vaguely uncomfortable, it was easier to let go.

- *No more wife*
- *No more children*
- *No more family*
- *No more memories*
- *No more... burdens*

One by one, as it were, the thick rope of my life unraveled until each single thread was exposed, tightened, and snapped.

And still I leaned into it.

Forgive me, but I can only describe it as *delicious.*

*We are not disturbed
by what happens to us,
but by our thoughts about
what happens to us.*

Eckhart Tolle

CHAPTER 3

LAZARUS, COME FORTH

Being awakened from dying was like the same natural violence that got me there. *But in reverse.*

After I let go of all perceived control over my brain activity, mobility, emotions associated with panic, and aspirations to live, I was comfortable.

That's yet another conundrum that caused me problems later.

The comfort was overwhelming, I suppose, because all of my struggles (like asthma) and all former activity (like brushing my teeth) had ended. So every aspect of my life was over, and I was *still* comfortable.

Think about pressures you find yourself under:

- *You've got a bill to pay*
- *You've got an image to uphold*
- *You've got an obligation to fulfill*
- *You've got a workout schedule to keep*
- *You've got a diet to follow*

Now imagine the pressure getting to be so much that you interrupt the pressure just to get a break:

- *Spend the money on something fun*
- *Screw what people think about you and let them know*
- *Don't show up or answer the phone*
- *Start exercising next week or month*
- *Stuff your face*

Remember that moment when the weight fell off your shoulders, the pressure disappeared, your brain relaxed, and everything got so quiet that you could actually pay attention to that hum in your ears?

That was me.

- *No cares*
- *No worries*
- *Beautiful*

NO FEAR
ONLY CURIOSITY

The best way for me to describe this next sequence of sensations is the following:

- *A loud quiet*
- *A dark room*
- *Curiosity*

Welcome Back, Lazarus

Insofar as sensations, I had no expectations of what happened to me, what was happening, or what was to come. And it didn't require any effort. I can only describe this state as curious:

- *I was aware that I was alone*
- *I was aware that it was "dark"—or, rather, that I didn't "know" what was happening*
- *I was curious because I could hear faint snatches of voices*

Yes, I heard voices.

But they weren't angels, or God, or even people to me. Whatever they were, I wanted to be there with them. I thought that if I concentrated my best and got quiet enough, I could hear what they were saying. And by hearing, I would be there with them.

I wasn't trying to get "back" anywhere. I just wanted to be with the source of all the noise.

WELCOME BACK, LAZARUS

But each time I felt myself getting closer and closer to the voices—without the aid of movement—I sensed myself approaching a threshold of sorts. I call it a "threshold" because each time I got close, I felt a warm sensation behind my eyelids as if I were being stirred by sunlight.

No, there was no literal light. But whatever stirred me would immediately disappear and I would find myself, as it were, back to where I started. The voices would be far away again, and I could only hear them by focusing. For some reason, I recall that this sequence happened at least a dozen times.

Then I was awake. And that's when the trouble began.

*Bird by bird, buddy.
Just take it
bird by bird.*

ANNE LAMOTT

CHAPTER 4

Aftermath

Robbie Grayson III

Here's the part of my experience that, forgive the pun, kills me. I had lost a little more than a day's worth of my life and awoke to no recollection of what happened to me. None.

- *That alarmed me*
- *That upset me*
- *That made me suspicious*

In other words for the entire time I was under, someone else made sure I breathed, was taken to the hospital, was intravenously fed, used the restroom (catheter), was medicated and monitored by professional medical staff, and had loved ones around me.

I couldn't do any of that on my own. So just as I needed all of that help, I needed people to tell me what happened to me:

- *Firsthand accounts by my wife and child who saved me*
- *The doctors and medical staff*
- *Secondary accounts by my other children and friends*
- *Dispatch (the 911 call)*
- *Hospital records*

I awoke, blinking my eyes. Several times. On the white wall opposite me were hanging objects. One was a clock, I believe. The more I blinked, the blurrier my vision became at first like the start of hard rain on a windshield while driving. When you turn the wipers on, one pass doesn't clear the windshield. But once you strike a rhythm, you can finally see well enough to move forward.

Maybe that's what a newborn baby feels like. I carried that same sense of ignorant wonder back into the world of the living.

Eventually, I could clearly see the items hanging on the wall but didn't know what they were. I wasn't thinking in terms of thoughts. I was still in the world of sensation where my cognition wasn't much help.

It just was what it was.

When I turned my head to the left, I saw the beautiful face of my wife. She was smiling from ear to ear and eagerly talking to me. But I couldn't hear or grasp fully what she was saying. I did catch the words, *Edith saved you. Do you remember?* I think that I picked this up by reading her lips and/or sensing what she was saying.

Whatever the case, I didn't immediately make the connection between what she said and why I was in a hospital bed.

Welcome Back, Lazarus

As I mentioned in the previous chapter, coming back is a definite violence in and of itself.

Remember, I had let go of everything I knew in a final sort of way. The individual threads of my life's rope had snapped in a way that I would *never* need them again.

But here I was again. Like a student who memorizes for a test and then forgets it all afterwards only to be told that the same questions will be on the final.

Damn.

The First Violence Was Language

Brain power was an energy from which I was free while under. For that entire time, anything I processed happened through sensation which—as best as I can describe—bypassed the brain.

Now that I was back, I fumbled with coordinating my brain energy with being conscious again. Language was virtually impossible and utterly exhausting. I couldn't understand what my wife was telling me or what her two friends—standing to my right—were telling me.

Each of their faces said more to me than their words, and I sensed that each was somehow responsible for my waking up.

I sensed that the doctor and nurses who tended me were anticipating violence from me. Whoever it was spoke to me slowly and deliberately as one would talk to a child. Not only could I not understand what he or she was saying, but I felt they were trying to ward off any sudden, aggressive move I would make. The approach agitated me, and the effort tired me.

Though they meant well, all I heard was the equivalent of little sirens that elevated my stress level which, coming from zero stress for almost 30 hours to the noise of life in a few minutes, felt like the beginning of anaphylaxis all over.

I didn't understand their words, but I felt as if the medical staff somehow wanted my cooperation. When I tried to speak back, I couldn't form a sound. I learned that I was intubated, which is a frightening ordeal while awake.

While I strangely had no gag reflex, saliva was pooling in the back of my throat and I thought I might drown.

Robbie Grayson III

The Second Violence Was Distraction

Perhaps, the tube down my throat made me feel superhuman. Perhaps, the sedation hadn't fully worn off. Whatever the case, I felt the need to demonstrate to everyone present that I was fully capable of breathing on my own.

Welcome Back, Lazarus

As I lifted my hands to signal to the medical staff, I realized that both hands were strapped to the sides of the bed. Momentarily, I became angry. I felt tricked—well, violated. More violated than when I realized that someone had stuck me with a catheter.

Was I seriously shaken from a deep, intoxicating sleep only to have to struggle like this again?

- *Failing to understand people*
- *Failing to identify things around me*
- *Being unable to move my hands*

In light of having my life back, these are little things. Easy things. Normal things, I guess. But each was the source of an incomprehensible rage.

Here is where my former sensibilities began to come back. I sensed the fear and suspicion of the medical staff and realized that I needed to put them at ease. Because their unease was making me uneasy. At this point, I became aware that whatever was happening was for my own good and that the medical staff wasn't going to pull the tube out or unstrap my hands any time soon,

I signaled to them with a slight head nod and finger gesture that I understood they were trying to help me.

The Third Violence Was Communication

Everything important that I tried to communicate in those first few minutes upon awakening was frustrated by the language barrier. Not only could I not understand what others were telling me, but I didn't know how to communicate back.

Granted, I had the tube down my throat and my hands were strapped. So I couldn't talk. But even then, I had no idea why I was in the hospital bed. I needed the people around me to tell me again and again *and again* why I was there until my brain fog cleared and it finally made sense.

Everything I had experienced over the previous day I had felt internally through strong physical sensations, their meanings only understood by me. The complexity of having so many people in the same room together with different energies, each trying to make themselves known through the normal act of communicating confused and angered me.

- *Why am I here?*
- *Who's in charge?*
- *Why can't I move?*
- *Is anyone listening to me?*
- *Are they hiding something from me?*

I still had no idea why I was confined to a bed.

My wife, God bless her, became my interpreter. She picked up that I felt I was drowning and negotiated to have my throat suctioned. When that result happened, I felt some hope that I could be understood.

Because my wife understood me, I thought that maybe I could try my hand at writing to express more complex ideas. So I pantomimed for a pen and some paper. My wife handed me an envelope and pen.

Communicating ended up being a failure and frustrating for me. As lucid as I thought I was and as slowly and carefully as I was forming my letters, not even my wife was able to make out much of what I was saying. The only sentence she was able to cipher—and she read it out loud—was something to the tune of *I thought I was in Valhalla, but they wouldn't let me in because I died of asthma.*

She and the others in the room were clueless about what that meant. So I decided to stop trying to explain myself until the medical staff took the tube out and unstrapped my hands.

WHAT DID I DO WRONG?

Someone eventually pulled the tube out of my throat and unstrapped my hands once the hospital determined that I had sufficiently come out of sedation and could control myself. When I found my voice, I must have been talking loudly to the people in the room, because a nurse appeared at my doorway, telling me to quiet down out of respect for the person in the room next to me. That person was dying. That's when I learned I was in ICU.

Shortly after, I began to remember bits and pieces of my crisis. I inquired of my wife specific questions about how I ended up in the hospital. I knew that there was no way that EMTs could have gotten to my house in enough time to save me from the time that I alerted her and my daughter. It was impossible, and it didn't make sense to me.

Welcome Back, Lazarus

My wife gave me the details:

- *My wife found me stumbling towards the bathroom*
- *I turned the faucet on cold, presumably to cool myself down*
- *I was biting down on the nebulizer*
- *My daughter called 911 on the phone*
- *I told my daughter to tell them to hurry because I only had 2 minutes left*
- *I collapsed into the shower*
- *The tension of the shower curtain rolled me onto the bathroom floor on my head*
- *I wasn't breathing*
- *My daughter conducted CPR on me*
- *The EMTs arrived*

After I let my wife's story soak in, I was seized by a sudden and uncontrollable shaking and sobbing that was beyond my ability to control.

The nurse on call eventually calmed me down, but I sat brooding in shame as other staff came in and out of the room throughout the day, taking sneak peeks at me and nervously asking me what I remember doing that might have caused me to end up in ICU.

Welcome Back, Lazarus

Initially, I was grateful to be alive. Especially while in the hospital, connected to the machines that kept me alive and monitored my progress. In fact, I was *overwhelmed* to be alive at first.

But for all that was done to save me, I was still having a hard time ciphering what people meant by the words they chose. There was too much to interpret and too much opportunity to get it all wrong. The underlying feeling I sensed was that people felt I was hiding a secret about why I was in this situation in the first place.

But how do you even begin to address a concern like that when you're not even one day old?

*Exit,
pursued by a bear.*

WILLIAM SHAKESPEARE

CHAPTER 5

BACK

I've said a couple of times already that the 30 hours I was under caused me problems later on. So it's time for me to explain what I mean.

Very quickly, all the morality, philosophy, and good manners to which I formerly ascribed was put to the test. By nature I'm diplomatic and friendly: flexible, long-suffering, and slow to judgment. But that changed.

Within a short period of time, I became the opposite of each. At times I wasn't sure why and at other times I wasn't aware of it.

The 1st Conundrum:
People Are Triggers

When I was aware of it, I didn't *want* to be difficult. I wasn't looking to take my anger out on people. I wasn't looking to avoid people. And I didn't think myself better than others.

In fact, I intentionally avoided contact, places where people were, and conversation altogether for one reason: *people triggered me.*

Robbie Grayson III

So, as ironic as it sounds, *people were the triggers.* I wish I could have said that back then had I understood it as clearly as I do now. It would have spared me accommodating everyone who wanted 1) to wish me well, 2) to ask me details about my situation, or 3) to generally "minister" to me. Most of these were takers who took what I didn't have to give:

- The *well-wishers* wanted to see if "the old Robbie" was back. That required me to comfort them.
- The *curious* wanted to hear obscure details I could recall. That required me to think hard.
- The *ministers* wanted to comfort me or give me space to "confess." That required me to play the victim or culprit.

After several energy-draining interactions with people I knew to be well intentioned, I didn't want anyone reaching out to me. Having been "under" for a little more than a day, I picked up on people's energy rather than their words. Most of the time, there was a differential that required more effort than I had to give in order to cipher what people really meant.

If you've ever had vertigo, an electric shock, or a sudden pounding headache, imagine doing your best not to show it on your face, in your voice, or in your overall demeanor. How long can you keep up the conversation?

If even for the best intentions you choose to dissociate like I did, something *has* to suffer. Instead of framing the conversation for others, I allowed them to frame it for me which meant that as externally friendly as I was with people, I was equally internally resentful of them as well.

First, I didn't want to believe that people *actually* believed the things that they said to me, as nice as they were trying to be.

- *God has a plan for you*
- *God needed you a little bit longer*
- *God's giving you another chance*
- *The Devil was testing with you*
- *The Devil is trying to stop you from...*

Second, I read angst into almost every comment. I felt that in a strange way most of the comments were clandestine warnings:

- *God has a plan, but do you know it?*
- *God needs you, but do you need God?*
- *You need to straighten up*
- *The Devil has your number*
- *You'd better figure this out real quick*

And all of this before I even left the hospital.

Robbie Grayson III

LEAVING
THE HOSPITAL

Welcome Back, Lazarus

The 2nd Conundrum: *No One Takes Me Seriously*

Several things unnerved me about leaving the hospital.

First, I don't remember arriving there.

Second, I was leaving ICU with no diagnosis of what happened to me and no assurance that it wouldn't happen again. Sure, the medical staff questioned me a number of times to get my take on why *I* thought I ended up there. They listened but challenged my diagnosis. In their opinion I was perfectly fine: no signs of asthma and no signs of anaphylaxis.

So after being discharged three days later, I felt I was hazarding danger. Who leaves ICU with nothing short of a diagnosis or outpatient care?

The only way I can explain my angst is to describe my life as an absurd cartoon.

Cartoons are funny for good reasons:

- *They take liberties with the real world*
- *No one gets permanently hurt*
- *The characters don't "get it"*

The ironies in a cartoon are exaggerated to the extent that they're ridiculous. I mean, when Wiley Coyote runs off a cliff, he can continue the forward motion in defiance of the law of gravity until he realizes that there's nothing beneath him. *Then* the law of gravity kicks in. Ha! But that's *not* how gravity works!

But that was now the new normal: *nothing is real if you don't acknowledge it.*

I felt like I was living *The Truman Show.* Everyone was tiptoeing around me, thinking that they were making the tiptoeing look natural. Except they weren't.

But they were serious.

But so was I.

And we both were seeing two completely different things.

Stalemate.

ROBBIE GRAYSON III

NATURE

Welcome Back, Lazarus

The 3rd Conundrum:
This World Is Not My Home

On the drive home from the hospital, everything outside seemed strange. Having been on my back for three days, standing or moving my head faster than my eyes could adjust gave me vertigo.

When they wheeled me out to the curb (hospital protocol), I inwardly cringed. It was overcast and humid outside. I felt it an ominous foreshadow of things to come and the paranoia set in:

- *I was overexposed*
- *If I stood up too fast, I would fall over*
- *People I didn't know could see me*
- *I thought my lungs would seize up*
- *I wouldn't be able to get away from the building fast enough if it decided to fall on me*

More than that, it hit me again that other than a preventative inhaler *the doctors didn't diagnose me with anything.* They didn't tell me what happened to me or offer theories why it might have happened. They were completely silent about that.

So my confidence in myself and others was at an all-time low. It was as if I were almost home free but still waiting for the other shoe to drop.

Welcome Back, Lazarus

The nurse who wheeled me out made small talk with me. He was on his way to Florida that weekend for vacation.

Dead man is what I thought. *You're going to die one day, you poor bastard, so enjoy your vacation.*

I tried to think differently, but I saw nothing but death imagery everywhere. When you have no faith in yourself for the future, you tend not to have faith for others as well. It was a disturbing way to start this new phase of my life, and I fought against it like I fought the anaphylaxis.

But *it* was winning.

My wife drove me home, and all I could do was stare out the window in wonder at the trees, grass, and hills. They were sinister. They contained within them poisons that made them appear to grow nice and lush but could kill a man, woman, or child if exposed to them in the wrong way.

The sun was shining, following the car, but I couldn't even look at it. It wasn't meant for me. I wasn't supposed to be here.

I was an alien. And ashamed of it.

Welcome Back, Lazarus

I stared at the car in front of us, keeping my eye on the shadowy figure behind the driver's wheel like I knew him.

He survived me, I thought. *And I don't even know his name. He's special. He made it.*

Robbie Grayson III

COMING HOME

Welcome Back, Lazarus

The 4th Conundrum:
When Home Feels Like a Tomb

As we pulled onto our long gravel driveway, I felt every familiar bump in the road with trepidation. The soybean fields surrounding our house had changed while I was gone, growing a few inches, and making the fields appear to hug our property more closely but in a vice grip.

When I walked into the house, I was greeted by my chaotic leaving:

- *My Last Will & Testament was out on the table in the foyer*
- *The house hadn't been cleaned*
- *No candles were lit*
- *No flowers were watered*

That wasn't a problem. It was enough for my friends and older daughters to keep the younger children occupied while I was in the hospital because my wife had stayed with me the entire time.

But when I walked into the bathroom, I tensed.

- *It looked like a fight had taken place*
- *The twisted shower curtain rod greeted me*
- *Paper from the defibrillator electrodes was torn and lying on the bathroom floor*
- *My broken nebulizer was on the sink with its tubing on the floor*

Here is where I died, and I didn't remember any of it.

The 5th Conundrum:
When Family Feels Like a Tomb

I'll briefly mention my family, because what others might have experienced with my new personality, my family experienced it more acutely.

My wife and I have six children and it was my 2nd-born who saved my life. She kicked my wailing wife out of the bathroom where I had lost consciousness and called 911 while giving me CPR that she had learned in her JROTC program just days before.

At the time, my second-born was pursuing a military medical career. As most responses to traumatic experiences tend to be delayed, my daughter struggled with anxiety for several months after which resulted in a domino effect of losses including the forfeiture of a full-ride Naval scholarship almost a year later.

My other children, who weren't as directly involved with my situation when it happened, either didn't directly inquire about what happened, got the important details secondhand from my wife or the sister who saved me, or otherwise didn't appear to take an interest in it. But they *were* interested.

However, "Children are the best recorders but the worst interpreters." And so it was with my own children. While they might have been fuzzy on the details of my "almost passing," the sum result was that each felt responsible for keeping me alive since I failed to do it on my own.

If I sneezed or coughed, my children would panic, showing up out of nowhere to inquire if I was OK. Sometimes, they would even periodically seek me out if they hadn't heard or seen me for some time. When they did, they would awkwardly ask, "How is your day going, Dad?"

Gratitude quickly turned into annoyance. Having six caretakers checking up on me several times a day felt like round-the-clock surveillance. These intrusions found me seeking solace for hours a day, sitting in my woodshed office or walking the fields around my house.

In psychology a child who takes on the role of the parent is a *parentified child.* My growing resentment towards my family found me acting like an *infantilized parent.* Was it isolation that I wanted or attention for isolating myself?

Welcome Back, Lazarus

I can't say enough about my wife. As the British say, she's a *brick.* A week before, we had celebrated our nineteenth wedding anniversary. Recovering from an incident like this one, however, was like being married to a stranger.

As nice and accommodating as my wife tried to be (as well as my children), the honeymoon period of being reunited lasted all but two weeks. By the end of that two week period, I found sleeping alone and milling around outdoors to be preferable. I wasn't sure why, but I couldn't look my wife in the face and had nothing of value to say as much as I tried.

The 6th Conundrum: *Did I Already Say "People Are Triggers"*

Immigrants, foster children, and newly released convicts feel similar to what I felt those first few weeks of being released from the hospital.

As soon as you're *released,* a lot of energy is burnt up in the excitable newness of "first contact."

- *new environment*
- *new people*
- *new experiences*

When things are new like this, they're enjoyable because of a simple, almost playful, appreciation of their surface features:

- *a new flower arrangement*
- *a new hairstyle*
- *a new flavor*
- *a new song*
- *a new smell*

Initially, a healthy amount of ignorance safeguards you from having to engage your higher reasoning which—if you use it prematurely—can burden your appreciation of new things by picking them apart.

So the honeymoon period of any new experience should have been all about the smiles. And it was.

When that honeymoon period is over, immigrants, foster children, and newly released convicts are now subject to the "deeper" meaning of things though they might not yet be ready for them. And if these deeper things are too many or too difficult for them, then they're faced with the prospect of making many mistakes (for which they will be corrected) or withdrawing.

So being home actually becomes uncomfortable.

Now, there was a huge difference between people who came to visit me at the hospital and house versus those who made phone calls and left voice mails, texts, and social media messages.

And while I was grateful for the show of support—even if a visit only lasted a few minutes (which I preferred) or a social media response was a LIKE—I was worried about conversation getting too "deep."

Getting "deep" meant that I had to listen to people's interpretations about my near-death experience and grade myself:

- *An evil spirit did this to me*
- *God did this to me*
- *I did this to me*

The problem I had with unsolicited advice was that I was still in a state of grief. Grief is intensely personal because it's felt and not thought. Most of the comfort people wanted to offer was faith statements, theological arguments, and pep talks intended to get me out of my funk.

While this all was appreciated in my "heart of hearts" because people let me know they cared, the problem is that each offering was language-based. What happened didn't happen to me because of language, so there was no way that enough language could get me out of it.

This factor was critical to my mental health at the time because I felt like some of my visitors were like Job's well-meaning friends who each wanted to spar with Job and get him to confess.

So I cut off a lot of these conversations. As many as I could anyway.

- *I ignored phone calls*
- *I ignored texts*
- *I ignored social media messages*

I ignored as much interaction as possible until some people stopped bothering me altogether. Though I understood that many of them meant well, each interaction was more stressful than helpful because I wasn't allowed to "be in my body."

Perhaps, one of the most authentic sentiments I felt during that time was from a combat vet who simply said, "That sucks."

Why the Drastic Personality Change?

While my behavior frustrated me as much as it frustrated others, it wasn't for the same reasons. Others wanted the "old" Robbie back because *Robbie* was a factor in their lives that no longer fit as he had before. The "new" *Robbie* didn't fit either. He was less sensitive, less patient, less friendly, etc. This situation was virtually true across the spectrum. When I sensed it, I was ashamed of it. At times I was embarrassed by it. I was sorry for it.

But I also didn't care.

Robbie Grayson III

Welcome Back, Lazarus

The body has a language all to itself, and that language isn't verbal. The body's language is sensual: that is to say, *of the senses.* If you stop thinking and talking long enough, you can "hear" your body speak to you. Your body will alert you that you've had enough to eat or that you're genuinely content. It will trigger you to pay attention to a physical discomfort long before it becomes a disease. It will signal you to take it easy when you're suddenly heavy with low energy that the mind calls anxiety or sadness.

If you believe verbal language to be the language of the body, you will squelch all that I just described to you. Your mind will tell you to control your body which means to ignore any sensation that doesn't align with the mind's terms or definitions.

Of all misunderstandings I've had with others who have asked about my near-death experience, this has been the deal-breaker.

This is where I've drawn a line many times since. In short, *it's better for my physical health that I be alone than among a group of people who ignore the language of the body in favor of the mind and expect me to act accordingly.* Verbal language like this becomes weaponized to deny the experience of the body.

When you're not functioning at your optimal self after an experience like that, loved ones want the "old you" back. But in the pursuit of helping you get "better," language becomes a tool to illustrate to "you" how far off you are from your former self.

I get it. I understood this better than a great number of the people wishing me well. And that was that I had traumatized others by my near-death experience. My close call made them uncomfortable and worry about their own mortality. So I needed to get better in order for them to feel better.

I get it.

*Is there a single person
on whom I can press belief?
No sir. All I can do is say,
'Here's how it went.
Here's what I saw.'*

LEIF ENGER

outro
where you go from here

After a two-week honeymoon period post-ICU, I isolated myself from my family for the better part of a month, spending most of that time in my little woodshed office, out in the yard, or out in the fields. How I spent my time, I couldn't tell you because each day was like one long trance.

One day about a month or so after coming home while sitting in my woodshed office, I decided I was done with the mood I was in. That I had to start wanting to live again. So I pulled out my iPhone, turned on the recorder, and started talking.

After 53 minutes and 21 seconds of stutter-stepping through fragmented memories in order to piece together a reason for the dark pit I was in, I stopped recording and gave it the title *Welcome Home, Lazarus!*

Dying isn't an easy thing to do, but coming back can be much harder. You can't unknow your own close call, and you can't ignore the conclusions that you draw deep inside yourself about it:

- *You're a miracle to all but yourself*
- *You're expendable and non-vital*
- *You wonder what you did to get here*

Most enigmatically, you have to die *again* one day and *that* time for good.

Using my own experience as an example, I want to offer three helpful practices you can use with those who you know have had close calls and aren't the same people anymore.

Affirm Their Experience

When you know that someone has had a brush with death, let them know that you know. It serves several purposes:

- *It affirms that it happened*
- *It affirms that others care*
- *It reinforces a gratefulness for life*

People unknowingly demean physical life by over-spiritualizing it, trivializing it, or taking it for granted. Physical life is important where physical life matters, and it's unimportant where it *doesn't* matter. Having a body and living in this physical world, however, matters. So there is no time that it *doesn't* matter.

Some people think differently, but the most final thing that can happen to a living organism is that it die. Because, physiologically-speaking, its physical life is over. And that includes all of its potential.

As a rule, I won't let my children kill bugs that make their way into our house (except hornets or some spiders, of course, if they can't help it), and I forbid them from killing the most insignificant creatures outside for the sport of it. That's just me, but it comes from a deeply disturbed place of knowing that when physical life is over, *that* form of life is done. No more potential in the same way. Forever.

Don't Sensationalize Their Experience

Close calls with death and dying are intensely personal. It's ignorant to ask a person to share the details of their experience for entertainment purposes or in order to offer one's own interpretation.

A close call might look fascinating in an artistic way to others. But to the one who experienced the close call, the sensations of powerlessness are embedded in the nervous system. When recollected, all of that nervous activity bubbles up: not in words (because oftentimes there were none) but in sensations.

People who provoke others like this don't appreciate the sorrow and grief that surrounds the personal loss of momentum. Even people in their right minds who are considered heroes by a fan base don't consider themselves heroes. If anything, focusing on the hero myth alienates them further. They end up privately reliving the fallout of that experience each time their "hero" status is mentioned.

If they want to share with you the details of a close call, they will. But if they do, it's almost always a gesture of trust and friendship more than an opportunity for them to teach you something or give you an opportunity to comment.

Don't Overwhelm Them with Anything: Including Love

Many who have experienced close calls tend to isolate themselves for one of many good reasons: *they don't want to talk.*

I didn't quite understand the reason for this until it happened to me. Our loved ones believe that the best way to demonstrate love is to be with us, to say the things they want to say before it's too late, to make up for lost time.

And much of that involves the medium of language. For me, a normally talkative person, the prospect of having to talk when I don't want to talk makes me want to go to bed and never wake up.

Dying is experienced at the somatic level: in the gut. Not in the brain. So the person struggling can't always verbalize what they're feeling. Talk is often unnecessary and a noise itself because now they have to figure out what you mean, why you said "that" word, or why you keep repeating the same words. It's cryptic, puzzling, and energy-sucking all at the same time.

If you have to ask questions, avoid the following as much as possible:

- Leading questions: *Are you feeling well?*, *Did you sleep OK?*, or *Are you in pain?* Such statements pose as yes & no questions with the intention to engage the other in conversation.

- Human function questions: *Are you hungry? Do you want a drink?* or *Would you like to be left alone?* Assume that the answer is always "yes" and just provide them with what you think they might want. But leave it where they can get it... without comment.

- Deep questions: *Did you hear the news? Do you want to tell me what you're thinking? Do you want to talk about it?*

When it comes to your wanting to engage in conversation, a more helpful approach would be to demonstrate what you want to say through any appropriate physical gesture that doesn't require the exchange of language. This is an important point, because silence for most people is considered rude.

Well, I advise that you keep your mouth closed for as long as you can stand it so long as your body language doesn't give the other mixed signals:

- *Touch (a hug, high five, pat on the back, etc.)*
- *Facial expressions (a smile, somber look, raised eyebrow, etc.)*
- *Gestures (a wave, thumbs up, head nod, etc.)*

If they can receive what you're offering without any sort of verbal explanation, you're doing a good job. When you do that, you're speaking their language. They get that *you* get where they are.

But more than anything else, they need to *feel* the comfort of another person. Comfort is the antidote to that conundrum they've experienced which was the temporary division of the soul from body. Because once you begin that descent into *The Valley of the Shadow of Death,* it opens only enough to make room for one person.

You.

CREDITS

QUOTES

p. viii. A.A. Milne, Author of the *Winnie the Pooh* series | *There are times when haggling over definitions doesn't contribute to a situation.*

p. 27. Lemony Snicket, Author of *A Series of Unfortunate Events* | *Science is to imperfection as the scientist is to toleration.*

p. 44. Eckhart Tolle. Author of *The Power of Now: A Guide to Spiritual Enlightenment* | *Being disturbed is a feature of the mind, not of the body.*

p. 57. Anne Lamott. *Bird by Bird: Some Instructions on Writing and Life* | *The smallest things in life are primary.*

p. 81. William Shakespeare | *This is an indirect way for a good guy to get rid of a bad guy.*

p. 118. Leif Enger. Author of *Peace Like a River* | *Personal truths can be accepted or rejected, but they aren't debatable.*

About the Author

Robbie Grayson III is the founder of Traitmarker and Traitmarker Books. He lives in Franklin, Tennessee with his wife and children.

Take the Free Assessment
www.traitmarker.com

Contact the Author
traitmarker@gmail.com

Get the Next Book
www.traitmarkerbooks.com

www.ingramcontent.com/pod-product-compliance
Lightning Source LLC
LaVergne TN
LVHW051927060526
838201LV00062B/4720